The Adventures of
Rocky

... the Kern Lodge Dog

I hope you Enjoy!

Phillis "Ann" Wirth

The Adventures of Rocky
... the Kern Lodge Dog
Copyright: 2018
Philla Sue Wiruth
All Rights Reserved

ISBN 978-0-359-15948-2

*This book is dedicated to all the parents of animals around the world and to all those that have gone out of their way to save defenseless
animals in their hour of need.*

Preface

Rocky the Lodge dog is a Labradoodle that came into my life, just when I needed a friend. At ten weeks old, he was already taller than most dogs and weighed in at 55 pounds. Over the years, Rocky has proved to be more than just a friend to me, he is now my constant companion and the love of my life. My Vet actually calls him my "Velcro dog" since he never leaves my side. All the stories you will read really happened. I hope that you will enjoy reading about my Rocky as much as I enjoyed writing his story. At the end of the book you will be introduced to Rocky's little brother, Rollie. My next book will be The Adventures of Rocky and Rollie. Look for it to come out soon.

In closing I would like to say, that this book came about because of a wonderful collaboration with my Illustrator, William Marlette. William guided me through the publishing maze with patience and has become a friend through the process. His Illustrations have brought Rocky to life.

"Lukie, I've decided to get a dog," said Sue to her 5-year old black cat. "A dog? Wait until Tiger Lily hears what you are planning. That German Shepard from next door nearly caught her the other day. How is she going to react when you bring a dog into our home?" responded Lukie. "This dog will be different. I will raise him to love the three of us," Sue responded, but inside, she was worried how Tiger Lily would react also.

"Oh, my boy! This carrier will never do. When did you get so tall?" chuckled Sandy as she looked at the puppy trying to get into the small carrier. "Guess I need to purchase an adult large dog carrier for you even at 9 weeks old!"

"Sue, I have some bad news. Your puppy won't be able to fly tomorrow as I had to take him to the Vet for a crushed paw. He was playing with my cow in the pasture and got stepped on. I'm so sorry. The Vet isn't sure if he will even be able to walk or not," sobbed Sandy as she relayed the sad story to Sue.

"Sandy, the puppy will be just fine. I already named him. His name is going to be Rocky. He is named after Saint Rocco, who is the patron saint for animals. Rocky will survive, and he will be able to walk and then run very soon. Please keep me informed of his progress. Thank you," said Sue as she hung up the phone and said a prayer that her puppy would heal quickly.

"Rocky, that's your new name by the way, you are going to be just fine according to the Doctor. I guess I am going to have to look up Saint Rocco," smiled Sandy as she guided Rocky into her car. "In another week we will get your stitches out and then you will be heading to California to your new home."

"Hi there little Rocky," said Skip as he pulled Rocky from his messy dog carrier. "Gosh you are a big puppy for 10-weeks old," grunted Skip, as he carried Rocky to a patch of fake grass to relieve himself after the long flight. It didn't take Rocky long for him to take the longest pee of his short life.

"This feels so good," relaxed Rocky as Skip cleaned all the pee and poo off his fur. "Time to dry your hair. A lot of dogs don't like this part, but I have a feeling you might just enjoy this," said Skip as he put Rocky into a space with warm blowers hitting him from all sides. Rocky looked at Skip as he was cleaning Rocky's crate and replacing the soiled bedding with wood chips. "You are right Skip, this is nice," responded Rocky as he laid down and enjoyed the warm air blowing on his wet fur.

"Who here is for the giant labradoodle?" asked Skip. The ladies looked at each other and asked among themselves who Skip was looking for. "OK, who here is for Rocky?" asked Skip again. "That would be me," said Sue excitedly. "Well then, you are here for the giant labradoodle! Rocky will be coming out on the Loading Dock in a few minutes."

Sue looked at Debra and said, "Giant Labradoodle? He didn't look that big on the internet." "Look at the size of the dog crate!" exclaimed Debra. "We will have to dismantle it to get it in the back of the Jeep!" Rocky looked through the crate and saw his new Mom. He smiled knowing that he was almost home.

"Debra, Rocky rolled the window down! Rocky, stay in the Jeep boy!" cried Sue as she pulled into a large parking area. But Rocky jumped out of the window as soon as the Jeep came to a stop. "Rocky, come back," yelled Sue as she ran after Rocky, who was running after a piece of trash blowing across the parking lot. Rocky thought that Sue was running after the trash too, so Rocky kept running thinking it was a game. Finally, Sue stopped and watched as Rocky got closer and closer to a busy main street.

"I thought I lost you boy. Please don't ever run off like that again," sobbed Sue into Rocky's freshly groomed fur. "You smell so good, Rocky. How is that possible after your long trip," asked Sue through her tears. "I'm sorry that I made you cry, Mom," Rocky said as he dropped the trash from his mouth. "I'll try not to make you cry ever again."

"Humph," grunted Debra. "I think he must be hungry. May I give him some hamburger now?" asked Debra. "Of course. He came a long way to become a part of our family," smiled Sue as she pulled out of the drive thru and onto the freeway to head to Kernville. Rocky ate until he was satisfied and then fell fast asleep in Debra's lap and stayed asleep for three hours until Sue pulled into the Kern Lodge, and Rocky's new home.

"We're home Rocky!" Rocky jumped out of the Jeep and looked around. "Right over there Rocky for the bathroom!" directed Sue as she guided Rocky to his new potty place. When Rocky was done, he smelled something he knew was not good. There was a cat close by and Rocky knew that cats were bad.

"Bark, Bark, Bark!" yelled Rocky as he got closer and closer to Lukie, as Lukie was swiping her full claws at Rocky's face. "Stop Rocky!" yelled Sue back at her new pup. "That's your sister!!" "What do you mean," responded Rocky with confusion, "She is a CAT!" "Yes, Lukie your older sister, is a cat. And so is your other sister, Tiger Lily," explained Sue as she pulled Rocky away from Lukie's swinging paws.

"Bark, Bark, Bark and it's not Lukie this time either!" yelled Rocky to Sue, who jumped out of bed to protect her cat, Tiger Lily. "Rocky, this is your other sister, Tiger Lily!" "Who is this?" hissed Tiger Lily as she swung her full claws at Rocky's nose. "This is your new little brother, Rocky," answered Sue. Just then, Rocky stopped barking and just stood there as Tiger continued to swing her paw closer and closer to Rocky's nose.

"You need to be nice to Tiger Lily. She has had a difficult life. I found her starving and suffering on the property as a 5 week-old kitten. Someone had kicked her and broken her sternum and she was hurting badly. The Veterinarian couldn't do anything about her broken chest bone except to give her pain medication. She doesn't trust humans and she doesn't like other animals, except for Lukie. Tiger needs your love, not your hate, Rocky," explained Sue to her young puppy, as she looked at Tiger with sympathy and concern.

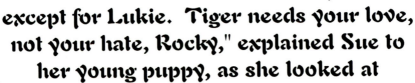

It was several months later in the afternoon, when Sue heard the barking of the Brewery's German Shepard getting closer and closer. Sue then saw Tiger Lily running across the driveway and gaining on her was the 120-pound German Shepard, Barley.

Sue was devastated as she could see that the Shepard was gaining on Tiger. With Tiger's injury to her chest bone, she couldn't run as fast as other cats.

Sue was just getting ready to yell at Barley, when she spotted Rocky on an intercept course with Barley. Seconds later Rocky ran right into the side of Barley, knocking him to the ground and Rocky with him.

Both dogs got up immediately and faced off for a few minutes. "Hey-Leave my sister alone!" yelled Rocky to Barley. "What?? Your sister?" smirked Barley. "She's a cat dude!" "Yep, and she is my sister, and so is Lukie, dude. You mess with them, you mess with me!" yelled Rocky as he was standing nose to nose with Barley, threateningly and showing his teeth. Rocky was so big for his age, that he was actually taller than Barley.

Barley realized, as he was standing nose to nose with Rocky, that Rocky was still a puppy. He also realized that as a puppy, Rocky was already taller than Barley. Barley figured that Rocky was going to be a big, big dog someday and Barley wanted to make sure that he was a friend with such a big dog and not an enemy.

Tiger Lily, breathing hard, as she looked down on the two dogs, realized that the only reason she was alive was because of Rocky. She couldn't believe it. Rocky the big dog came to her rescue. " If you can't play nice, then get off our property and go back to the Brewery where you belong," barked Rocky. Barley looked up at Tiger Lily for the final time and then glanced back to Rocky. Ever so slowly, Barley turned around and headed back to the Brewery property next door.

Rocky watched until Barley reached the
Brewery property, and then Rocky looked
up at Tiger Lily to make sure she was
OK. Tiger just stared at Rocky. Not only
did he stop Barley, but Rocky had actually
saved her. Tiger knew that she wouldn't
have made it to the block wall and to
safety in time, without Rocky's
intervention.

"What did you do that for?" hissed Tiger, not wanting to show Rocky that she really appreciated what he did for her. "I'm your brother. That's what family does. We stand up for each other," responded Rocky. After he had said that, he laid down at the base of the block wall until Tiger was ready to come down.

"I never had anyone protect me before and I certainly never had a dog for a friend," hissed Tiger. But as she was saying it, she quieted down her hissing and took a seat next to Rocky. "I guess you want me to say, 'thank you' but I really think I could have made it to the wall without your help," continued Tiger Lily. But deep down, Tiger knew she wouldn't have made it to safety without Rocky's help. Rocky just looked at Tiger with love. "Well, thank you, Bro," said Tiger finally as she continued to sit next to Rocky.

Tiger never brought up the subject again,
but ever since that day,
Tiger would follow Rocky around the
property. When Rocky lay down, so would
Tiger Lily a few feet from Rocky. When
Rocky ran after other cats and dogs on the
property, Tiger would watch from a safe
place until all was safe again.

"Hey, wait up for me!" called Tiger to Rocky as she ran to catch up with her big brother. "I could tell you were there," responded Rocky, "as your bell around your neck gives you away." "I know, it's annoying. It's hard to sneak up on mice with this thing around my neck," laughed Tiger. Rocky couldn't help but love his little "older" sister, even if she was a cat. Tiger started following Rocky everywhere after that day. They became known as Rocky and his little shadow.

One day, Sue was alone at work and couldn't watch Rocky. "Rocky, I need to put you in the pool area so you don't run off the property. No one is here today to watch you and I have to do some work at the office. You can play and have fun in here, just don't go in the water because it's cold right now," warned Sue as she directed Rocky into the Pool area. Sue shut the gate to the pool area and Rocky watched her walk away as he gazed through the chain link fence.

Rocky looked around and saw a large blue-ish floor and lots of dirt and flowers all around. Rocky started to run. He loved to run. After a while he was running so fast that he lost his footing and fell into the blue-ish floor.
Only it wasn't a floor at all!

"Help! Help!" yelled Rocky. "I'm being swallowed up by this wet stuff!" Rocky thought for sure he was going to drown because he didn't know how to swim. "Help! Help! Please!" Rocky continued yelling. All of a sudden, a man jumped into the blue-ish stuff (which I now know is a Pool!) and saved me! "Thank you so much, Lick, Lick, Lick," Rocky said to the man. "Good thing I was watching you running around in circles my little friend, otherwise you might have been in the pool a long time!" said the man.

"Let's go find your Mom," said the man with a soothing voice. The man was carrying Rocky in his arms, dripping wet. The man went to the office and found Sue working there. When Sue saw that Rocky was soaking wet, she panicked and ran up to the man, who was also soaking wet and took Rocky into her arms. "What happened?" asked Sue to the nice man who was a guest of the Lodge. The man explained how Rocky was running round and round the pool and then slipped and fell in the deep end. Sue was saddened to think that Rocky may have succumbed to drowning in the pool because she left him in the area alone.

"Thank you so much," cried Sue as she pulled Rocky close to her. The man patted Sue on the back and left her alone with her dog. " I'm so sorry Rocky. Just thinking that I might have lost you because of a stupid mistake on my part. I should have known that you were just a puppy and didn't know about water yet," Sue said sadly.

" It's OK Mom. The nice man told me you were a good person and that you didn't mean to hurt me. Besides, I fell in the pool, I wasn't pushed. But I wouldn't mind getting a treat for being all wet...," hinted Rocky. He smiled at Sue, but inside of Rocky, he was shaking with fear. He never wanted to get near the blue-ish water again. Ever again.

"Rocky, don't you want to come into the water?"
Sue asked, as the summer rolled around the
following year. "Nope, I'm good here watching
you from the side, Mom" responded Rocky. He
never wanted to get into that pool again. He
remembered that he nearly drowned last winter
and he wasn't going to go into that water ever
again. Time after time that summer, Sue tried to
get Rocky into the pool, but each time Rocky ran
to the far corner of the pool area to get away
from the water.
Sue felt bad that Rocky was a water dog who
was so afraid of water because of a mistake
that Sue had made when he
was a puppy.

The following summer it was so hot in
Kernville and Sue couldn't exercise Rocky by
running him normally, so Sue decided that
she had to get Rocky into the water to
exercise him. "Look Rocky, I bought you a
Life Jacket!" said Sue excitedly to Rocky as
she fitted the bright yellow jacket around
Rocky's midsection.
"What is this for?" asked Rocky. "This is
going to make you float when we go swimming
in the river!" explained Sue with excitement
in her voice. Rocky just looked at his Mom.
"River, what the heck was she talking about?
What was a river?"

Sue told Rocky to get into the Jeep and without hesitation, Rocky jumped into the vehicle. Whatever this river was, as long as it meant taking a ride in the Jeep, Rocky was all for it. River here we come! But after a ten minute ride, Rocky had a change of heart, as Sue pulled up beside a body of water that was moving. "Ah," thought Rocky, "now I know what a river is, it's another form of the wet stuff that nearly drowned me when I was a puppy. Not going to happen Mom!"

"OK Rocky, here we are at the river. This is the Kern River. And we are going to swim here. Come on now. Walk with me," as Sue tried to gently guide Rocky down to the river. But Rocky had already decided he would have nothing to do with it and put the brakes on and sat down in the dirt. Sue, however had also decided that she was not going to take 'no' for an answer and just continued dragging Rocky down to the water, all the while talking to him.

"You are going to like the water Rocky. I know that you didn't like it at first when you were a puppy, but you will like it today. It will feel nice in this heat and you will float with your bright yellow vest on. You will see. You will have fun," encouraged Sue. Sue dragged Rocky all the way into the water until suddenly Rocky was floating. The look on Rocky's face was priceless. It was a look of shock and of happiness all at once. He started to doggie-paddle and he was having FUN. "Hey, this is nice mom! I do like it! And it's cool in here!" said Rocky with a big smile on his face.

The next day, Sue took Rocky to the same place again. This time Rocky resisted but Sue didn't have to drag him quite as hard to get him into the water. Rocky was still a little afraid of getting into the water, but after another fun day of swimming, Rocky decided that if his Mom brought him back here again tomorrow, that he was going to show her that he WAS a water dog after all! The third day was the greatest day in Rocky's and Sue's swimming memories. As soon as Sue opened the back of the Jeep, Rocky leapt from the back of the Jeep and ran into the water. Sue just laughed and ran after him.

For the rest of the summer, Sue and Rocky could be found playing in the Kern River and Rafters would often float by and call out to Rocky the Lodge dog in the bright yellow life vest, "Hello Rocky! What a great water dog you are!!"

"Mom, there is no one to play with when you are working all day," complained Rocky. "Sorry Rocky, you will just have to entertain yourself. But don't leave the property. I need to work in the office to take care of our guests," responded Sue to her bored little boy. "OK Mom. I'll try to find something to keep me busy until you are available to play with me," sighed Rocky as he tried to figure out something to entertain himself.

"Rocky? Rocky? Where are you?" Sue yelled as she walked around the property. Just then, Sue's cell phone rang. "Sue, do you own a big black dog named Rocky?" "Yes, is he OK?" asked Sue. "Rocky is just fine, but our guests down here at the Pizza Barn are not as fine, as Rocky is going from table to table begging for food!" responded the upset owner, Brad. "Oh, I am so sorry! I will be right there to get him!" "Bad boy Rocky!" scolded Sue when she finally got ahold of Rocky's collar. "You mean that the Pizza Barn isn't on our property Mom?" asked Rocky in confusion. "No, Rocky. The Pizza Barn is not on Kern Lodge property!"

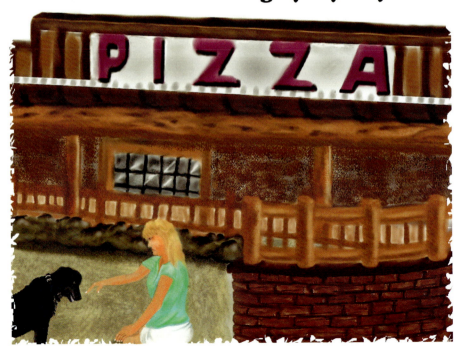

A week later Sue again couldn't find Rocky and was calling all around the property for him, "Rocky, Rocky? Where are you?" when the phone in her pocket rang. "Hi Sue, this is Mrs. Delap, the Principal at the Elementary School across the street. Your dog Rocky is over here in the playground playing with the kids. And although the kids are having fun with him, I don't think that all the parents would be happy to see such a large dog playing with their kids," chided the principal.

"Bad boy Rocky!" scolded Sue once again as she grabbed Rocky's collar and again dragged him back to the Lodge property. "So, this isn't part of the Lodge property either?" questioned Rocky as Sue was pulling him by the collar. "No, Rocky. Not here and not the Pizza Barn!" yelled Sue back, embarrassed that she had to retrieve Rocky away from the children. "But the children liked me Mom, why are you so mad at me?" asked Rocky. "Because I told you not to leave the property and you did anyway!" yelled Sue back to Rocky.

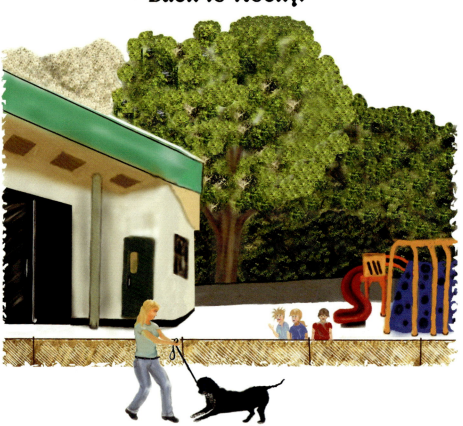

It was the very next day, when again
Rocky went missing. "Sue, this is
Rebecca at the Brewery. Rocky is over
here on the patio pestering people for
food." "I am so sorry Rebecca. I guess I
am going to have to figure out something to
keep Rocky on the property."
Sue responded sadly as she started
walking over to retrieve her wayward
boy once again.

"Rocky, what am I going to do with you? Why don't you want to stay on the property?" asked Sue. "Sometimes it's lonely here. And when it is, then I like to go to the Brewery or the Pizza Barn or the School to play with friends," responded Rocky. "Then I guess it's time that I get you a little brother," smiled Sue as she snuggled up to Rocky.

"Mom, what is this white fuzzy thing?" asked Rocky. "That is your new little brother, Rollie." "But he is the size of a toy! How can I play with him?" cried Rocky. "Just be a little patient. Someday very soon, he will be bigger than you," smiled Sue as she drove Rocky and Rollie back to their home at the Kern Lodge.